Stress *to* Serenity

The Art of Stress Free Living

Dr. Rekha Gaur

BlueRoseONE.com
Stories Matter
NewDelhi • London

BLUEROSE PUBLISHERS
India | U.K.

For permissions requests or inquiries regarding this publication, please contact:

BLUEROSE PUBLISHERS
www.BlueRoseONE.com
info@bluerosepublishers.com
+91 8882 898 898
+4407342408967

ISBN: 978-93-7310-319-8

Cover design: Aman Sharma
Typesetting: Manisha Rawat

First Edition: November 2025

Dear Reader,

Stress is something I have witnessed not only around me but also within myself, at different stages of life. Like you, I have faced moments of doubt, pressure, and exhaustion—times when the weight of responsibilities seemed heavier than my strength. It is in those very moments that I realised: stress does not speak, but the body always listens.

This book is born out of both my personal experiences and professional understanding. As I worked with people and observed the challenges of modern life, I felt a strong need to create a guide that is not complicated or distant, but simple, practical, and relatable. A book that does not just explain what stress is, but shows how one can gently walk from stress toward balance, peace, and inner strength.

Every chapter you will read here is written with the intention of being a companion—not a lecture. You will find methods, reflections, and exercises that you can practice in your daily routine without difficulty. More importantly, I hope you will find comfort in knowing that you are not alone.

I dedicate this work to all those who strive every day to hold themselves together in the rush of life. May this book be a small light on your journey, reminding you that change is always possible, and peace is always within reach.

With warmth and hope...

Dr. Rekha Gaur

Preface

In today's fast-paced world, stress has become an uninvited companion in almost every individual's life. It slowly creeps into our daily routine, silently affecting our mental clarity, emotional balance, and physical health. Over time, it weakens relationships, reduces our capacity to work efficiently, and steals away the simple joys of living.

This book has been written with a simple purpose: to provide every person struggling with daily challenges a path that is practical, compassionate, and deeply human. Stress cannot always be eliminated, but it can be understood, managed, and transformed. With awareness and the right approach, what once felt like a burden can become a stepping stone toward resilience and inner peace.

Unlike books that merely describe theories, this work is intended to be a journey of self-discovery and healing. It blends practical techniques with reflective insights so that readers can not only learn about stress but also actively apply strategies in their everyday lives.

The chapters of this book explore:

The effects of stress on health, relationships, and productivity.

Principles of stress management, including acceptance, balance, and time mastery.

Simple yet effective practices like deep breathing, exercise, yoga, and mindful living.

The power of positive self-talk and inner dialogue.

The healing role of social support and meaningful communication.

I Hope, as you turn the pages, you will find not just information but also inspiration—a gentle reminder that you are not alone in your struggles. Stress is not the end of the road; it can be the beginning of transformation. With patience and practice, every individual has the ability to create a life that is healthier, calmer, and more joyful.This book is, above all, an invitation—to pause, to breathe, to reflect, and to rediscover the strength that already lies within you.

Introduction

Stress has become an inseparable part of modern life. Whether it is the pressure of deadlines, financial responsibilities, relationship challenges, or simply the fast pace of the world, we all encounter moments when life feels overwhelming. Stress may not be visible like a wound or an illness, but its impact is often deeper and more lasting—it affects how we think, how we feel, how we work, and even how we connect with others.

Yet, it is important to remember that stress is not always an enemy. In small amounts, it can motivate us, push us to grow, and prepare us to face challenges. The real problem arises when stress becomes constant and unmanaged. Prolonged stress begins to drain our energy, disturb our health, and rob us of the joy of living. It is this kind of stress that this book addresses—the stress that weighs us down rather than lifting us up.

This book is not a medical manual or a theoretical discussion. It is designed as a practical guide and companion, offering you simple methods, reflections, and real-life strategies to manage stress in ways that fit naturally into daily life. You will find a blend of psychology, wellness practices, and mindful living techniques—presented in a style that is easy to understand and apply.

The chapters are structured to take you step by step:

First, by helping you understand what stress is and how it impacts your body, mind, and relationships.

Then, by exploring principles and practices that allow you to manage stress effectively.

And finally, by guiding you toward building long-term resilience, so that you are not just fighting stress, but transforming it into a pathway toward balance, growth, and inner peace.

Think of this book as a journey. Each chapter invites you to pause, reflect, and take small but meaningful actions. You do not need to rush; progress comes through gentle consistency. Even if you apply just one idea at a time, you will begin to notice a shift—more calmness, more clarity, and a deeper sense of control over your life.

Remember, stress will always exist in some form. But how we respond to it is within our power. This book is here to remind you of that power and to encourage you to use it.

So, as you begin reading, I invite you to keep an open mind and an open heart. Take what resonates with you, practice it in your daily routine, and allow yourself the space to heal and grow. This is not the end of your struggles—it is the beginning of a new way of living.

Welcome to your journey— from stress to solution.

📖 Table of Contents

🏵 Understanding Stress

🕊 "तनाव को समझना ही उसे हल करने की पहली सीढ़ी है।"

"Understanding stress is the first step towards resolving it."

Prompt: Recall one situation where you felt stressed. Was it your reaction or the situation itself that created the pressure?

Discover what stress really is, how it originates, and why it affects people differently. This chapter lays the foundation for recognizing stress as more than just "pressure" but as a physical, mental, and emotional response.

🏵 The Effects of Stress on Daily Life

🌸 "छोटा सा तनाव, बड़ा असर छोड़ सकता है।"

"Even small stress can leave a big impact."

Prompt: Which part of your life—health, work, or relationships—do you feel stress affects the most?

Explore how unmanaged stress impacts health, work efficiency, relationships, and emotional well-being. Learn to identify the hidden costs of carrying stress silently.

🏵 The Science of Stress

🍃 "शरीर कभी झूठ नहीं बोलता, तनाव को वह हमेशा सुनता है।"

"The body never lies; it always listens to stress."

Prompt: Notice your body when you are tense. Where do you feel it the most—head, chest, stomach, or elsewhere?

A simple explanation of how stress affects the brain, nervous system, and body. Understand the role of hormones, triggers, and the body's "fight or flight" response.

Principles of Stress Management

"स्वीकार करना, बदलना, और संतुलित रहना ही शांति का मार्ग है।"

"Acceptance, change, and balance are the true path to peace."

Prompt: Which principle do you find harder—acceptance, adjustment, or time management?

Why?

Learn guiding principles—acceptance, adaptability, balance, and time management—that serve as the cornerstones for living with greater peace and control.

Practical Techniques for Everyday Life

"छोटे कदम, बड़े बदलाव ला सकते हैं।"

"Small steps can create big changes."

Prompt: What one small practice—deep breathing, walking, or journaling—can you start today?

Discover easy-to-use tools such as deep breathing, yoga, exercise, and meditation. Practical steps that can be woven into your daily routine without disruption.

Positive Self-Talk and Emotional Healing

"जैसा आप खुद से कहते हैं, वैसा ही आप बनते हैं।"

"You become what you repeatedly tell yourself."

Prompt: Write down one negative thought you often repeat. How can you reframe it into a positive statement?

Understand the power of your inner dialogue. Learn how affirmations, hopeful thinking, and self-compassion can reshape the way you deal with challenges.

The Role of Relationships and Social Support

"बातें साझा करना, बोझ हल्का करना है।"

"Sharing your feelings lightens the burden of stress."

Prompt: Who is the one person you feel safe talking to? How often do you reach out to them?

Find out how family, friends, and community can be powerful allies in reducing stress. Learn the importance of sharing, listening, and building meaningful connections.

Building Inner Resilience

"मजबूती समस्याओं से बचने से नहीं, उनका सामना करने से आती है।"

"Strength comes not from avoiding problems, but from facing them."

: Think of a challenge you overcame in the past. What inner strength helped you through it?

Go beyond quick fixes. This chapter teaches you how to strengthen your inner capacity to handle setbacks, cultivate optimism, and bounce back stronger.

A 21-Day Stress-Free Journey

"हर दिन एक नया अवसर है परिवर्तन लाने का"

"Each day is a fresh opportunity to begin change."

Prompt: What one habit can you commit to practicing consistently for the next 21 days?

A guided, step-by-step program designed to help you practice small daily actions for lasting change. A simple, practical roadmap to reduce stress in just three weeks.

From Stress to Solution: A New Beginning

The closing chapter brings together the lessons of the book, offering encouragement, reflection, and a vision for living a calmer, more joyful, and stress-free life.

"Towards a Simple Journey to a Stress-Free Life"

Contents

Understanding Stress – The First Step to Solutions

1. Introduction: Stress in Today's World

In today's fast-paced, connected world, stress has quietly become an unwelcome companion. From juggling work deadlines to family responsibilities and social expectations, stress touches every aspect of life. Unlike a visible injury or illness, it often develops silently, affecting mind, body, and relationships without warning.

Anecdote:

Consider Riya, a young professional in a bustling city. She wakes up at 6 A.M. rushes to work, manages multiple projects, and returns home exhausted. Even during leisure, she worries about pending tasks. Riya thinks this is normal—but in reality, her body and mind are signalling stress.

2. What is Stress?

Stress is the body and mind's natural response to challenges or demands. Not all stress is harmful. Small amounts, called eustress, can motivate us to achieve goals, meet deadlines, or face challenges. Chronic or overwhelming stress, known as distress, negatively affects health, relationships, and overall life satisfaction.

Illustration idea: A dashboard warning light analogy: occasional flashes are helpful alerts; constant flashing signals danger.

3. Causes of Stress

External Causes:

Deadlines, workplace pressure, conflicts

Family responsibilities, relationship challenges

Major life changes: moving, financial shifts, loss of loved ones

Internal Causes:

Self-criticism, perfectionism, unrealistic expectations

Fear of failure or judgment

Negative thoughts and unresolved emotions

Case Study:

A 14-year-old student, Aarav, feels anxious before every exam. His parents unknowingly increase pressure, asking for top marks. Aarav's stress is a mix of internal expectations and external pressure—demonstrating how stress affects even young minds.

4. How Stress Affects the Mind

Chronic stress impacts emotional and cognitive functioning:

Anxiety: constant worry

Irritability: frequent frustration

Depression or sadness: loss of motivation

Cognitive difficulties: poor focus, forgetfulness

Mini Exercise:

List situations in the past week that caused irritation or worry. Notice patterns—this helps identify stress triggers.

5. How Stress Affects the Body

Stress activates the body's **"fight or flight"** response, releasing hormones like cortisol and adrenaline. Long-term effects include:

Headaches, tension in muscles

Sleep disturbances

High blood pressure and rapid heartbeat

Digestive issues

Anecdote:

Sanjay, a middle-aged office worker, started experiencing frequent headaches and digestive problems. Only after keeping a journal did he realize that his stress from unresolved work conflicts was causing physical symptoms.

6. Stress and Relationships

Stress changes how we interact with others. Stressed individuals may withdraw, become irritable, or communicate poorly. This impacts:

Family life: arguments with partners or children

Workplace: strained teamwork, decreased collaboration

Case Study:

Meera, under constant work stress, snapped at her friend during a casual conversation. Reflecting later, she realized it wasn't personal—her stress had influenced her behaviour. Awareness allowed her to apologize and manage her reactions better.

7. Signs You Might Be Stressed

Persistent fatigue

Mood swings

Difficulty making decisions

Loss of interest in hobbies

Physical symptoms: headaches, rapid heartbeat

Reflection Exercise:

Keep a daily log of physical and emotional signs of stress. Identify patterns over two weeks.

8. The Cost of Ignoring Stress

Ignoring stress can have consequences:

Physical: heart problems, weakened immunity

Emotional: Anxiety, Depression

Social: strained relationships, Isolation

Professional: burnout, mistakes

ILLUSTRATION IDEA:

A tree with roots representing ignored stress, eventually causing the trunk (life) to crack—visual metaphor for long-term effects.

9. Stress as a Signal, Not the Enemy:

Stress is a signal, not a foe. It alerts us that something in life needs attention or change. By recognizing this, we shift from being victims to problem-solvers. Stress can be the first step toward growth and better habits.

Anecdote:

Vikram, a software engineer, often felt overwhelmed. By interpreting stress as a signal rather than a burden, he organized his tasks, delegated responsibilities, and adopted mindfulness practices. Gradually, he transformed stress into motivation.

10. Reflection and Awareness Exercises

1. **Journaling:** Record situations causing stress and reactions.

2. **Self-rating:** Daily stress scale of 1–10.
3. **Mindful Observation:** Notice body sensations during stress—tight shoulders, rapid heartbeat.
4. **Mini Meditation:** Spend 5 minutes focusing on breathing when noticing stress.

Illustration idea: Simple diagram showing stress → awareness → action → relief.

11. Summary & Key Takeaways

Stress is natural; chronic stress is harmful.

Causes include external pressures and internal thought patterns.

Stress affects the mind, body, and relationships.

Early recognition prevents long-term consequences.

Stress can be reframed as a signal for growth.

Awareness is the first step. By noticing stress, we open the door to solutions. This chapter sets the foundation for the journey toward a stress-free life, which will be explored in the following chapters.

Causes of Stress: Internal and External

"Every stress has a source, but we often don't want to recognize it."

Stress is like a guest who comes without an invitation and stays for a long time. We often feel that we are under stress, but we fail to understand where it actually comes from.

External Causes (External Stressors)

1. Workplace stress:

*Difficulty in completing tasks.

*Lack of support from the boss or colleagues.

*Job insecurity.

*Competition for promotion.

Motivational Example-

Mahendra was a hardworking employee, but when three of his team members left him, the burden of work fell entirely on his shoulders. He suffered from headaches and confusion every day. Due to the workload, he also developed the problem of insomnia.

2.Financial Problems –

*Worries about monthly financial expenses

*Debt

*Insecurity about the future

*Children's education and marriage

Ask yourself: Is the source of your worries only the uncertainty of money?

3.Family responsibilities

*Children's education

*Harmony in relationships

*Caring for the elderly

*Illness of a family member

All of these can become sources of stress.

Motivational Example....

Neera was a homemaker. But when her mother-in-law fell seriously ill and her husband was transferred, she began to feel mentally exhausted. She could not express her struggles to anyone, yet there was a constant turmoil within her.

4.Relationship stress –

Disagreements between husband and wife, growing distance between parents and children, family conflicts, divorce or separation—all of these deeply affect a person's mental well-being.

Emotional imbalance often becomes the deepest root of stress.

Motivational Example

Radhika and Arun had been married for ten years. Over time, small disagreements turned into frequent arguments. Radhika often felt that Arun did not understand her emotions. Their children sensed the growing distance between their parents, which created an atmosphere of tension in the entire family.

Radhika began to experience anxiety and sleepless nights The emotional imbalance in their relationship not only strained their bond but also became a significant source of stress for the whole household.

5.Social Media and the Web of Comparison –

*Looking at the seemingly "perfect and successful" lives of others on social media often creates dissatisfaction in one's own life.

*The constant chase for likes and followers.

Along with digital fatigue, has become a modern form of stress. When you begin comparing yourself with everyone, your self-confidence weakens, and inner mental exhaustion silently increases.

Self-question: Do you compare yourself with everyone around you?

Internal Causes (Internal Stressors)

These are causes that arise from our own way of thinking.

1. Negative Thinking –

thoughts like "I will never succeed"

*Always expecting the worst in every situation.

*Lack of self-belief.

Inspirational Note:

The world appears the way you choose to see it. This is not just a proverb, but also a truth supported by science.

Self-question:

Do you often expect the worst in every situation instead of believing in your own potential?

2. Lack of Self-dialogue –

*When a person does not communicate with themselves

* suppresses their emotions, and becomes too harsh on their own efforts

* stress slowly builds up inside.

* The inability to express joy or pain often creates inner restlessness and emotional imbalance.

Self-question:

When was the last time you truly laughed with an open heart?

3. Perfectionism –

*Expecting 100% in every task or conversation

*Treating mistakes as failures

*Forgetting yourself in the constant race to be the best.

These are deep sources of stress.

Motivational Example:

Sandhya was a school teacher who always wanted to deliver her very best in every class. Over time, her health began to decline, and she started feeling constant fatigue.

Yet, she could not recognize the heavy burden of perfectionism she was carrying within herself.

Self-question:

Do you push yourself so hard to be perfect that you forget to care for your own well-being?

4. Fear and Insecurity –

*Worries about the future

*Fear of being left alone

*Thoughts like "What if this happens?"

often weaken us from within.

The truth is that almost 90% of our fears are based on imagination, not on reality.

Self question:

"Is this fear based on reality, or is it just a product of my imagination?"

5. Unfulfilled desires and regrets –

*The ache of not having done something

*Thoughts like 'I wish I had…'

*we often live in the past even today.

Please understand Our mind is either trapped in what has already happened or tangled in worries about the future, and as a result, we lose the peace of the present."

Self question:

"Am I living in the present, or am I letting the past and future steal my peace today? "How to identify the causes of stress?

***Start with a diary...**

Every day, before going to bed, spend five minutes writing. Reflect on: What happened today? How was my day? Who or what caused me the most stress?"

Self-reflective question:

"What specific events or interactions today triggered my stress, and why did they affect me so strongly?"

***Start with 'Why'?**

For every stress or problem, ask 'Why?' five times and answer yourself.

For example:

I feel stressed. Why?

→ Because my meeting didn't go well.

Why?

→ Because I wasn't properly prepared.

Why?

→ And continue asking further in the same way..."**

Self-reflective question:

"What underlying reasons keep causing this stress, and how can I address the root cause rather than just the surface issue?"

***Understand the language of your body....**

If you have a headache, digestive issues, or insomnia, pay attention to the state of your thoughts and mental well-being."

Self-reflective question:

"What thoughts or worries might be causing my body to react this way, and how can I address them?"

✨ Self-Reflection Prompts (Workbook Style)

1. Body Signals

What signals does my body give me when I am under stress?

✍ My answer: ______________________________

2. Impact on Life

How does my stress affect my work, relationships, and daily routine?

✍ My answer: ______________________________

3. Rest & Recovery

Do I allow myself enough time to rest and recharge? If not, why?

✍ My answer: ______________________________

4. Self-Blame

Do I blame myself unnecessarily for everything?

✍ My answer: ______________________________

5. Expectations

What are my true expectations—from myself and from others?

✍ My answer: ______________________________

Reflection note:

"Knowing the beginning of stress is the first step to dealing with it. By identifying it early, you can understand its direction and prevent it from growing further. If you become aware at the right time, you will be able to remain healthy and balanced."

Effects of Stress on Body and Mind

Stress can neither be seen nor heard, yet the body and mind deeply experience it. It quietly influences our thoughts, emotions, and health—like an invisible weight that drains us and takes away our balance.

"Stress is often taken lightly—

'It's just a little tension, a normal thing, everyone goes through it.'

But when this stress is ignored for a long time, it gradually begins to leave a deep impact on both the body and the mind."

1. Effects of Stress on the Body

*Impact on the Heart:

Rapid heartbeat and increased blood pressure

Prolonged stress can increase the risk of heart attack or stroke

Cholesterol imbalance and disrupted blood circulation

*Anger and Blood Pressure:

People who get angry frequently may experience fluctuating blood pressure

***Effects of Stress on the Digestive System:**

Stress can cause heartburn, gas, and constipation.

It may lead to reduced appetite or, in some cases, overeating.

The stomach is closely connected to the brain and is often referred to as the "second brain."

***Effects of Stress on the Immune System:**

Weakening of the immune system

Frequent colds and infections

Reduced ability of the body to fight infections

Slow healing of wounds.

***Effects of Stress on Muscles and Bones:**

Pain in the neck, shoulders, and back

Muscle tension and stiffness

People under stress often clench or grind their teeth, a condition known as bruxism.

***Effects of Stress on Sleep Quality:**

Difficulty falling asleep(Insomnia)

Frequent waking during the night

Disturbing dreams or nightmares

Restless or unsatisfying sleep

***Effects of Stress on Skin and Hair :**

Hair problems such as hair loss or premature greying

Skin issues like acne, rashes, or allergies

Skin discoloration or dullness.

2. Effects of Stress on the Mind

***Anxiety disorders**

Constant worry

Feeling nervous or restless all the time

Increased heart rate without any apparent reason

Fear of public places or social situations (agoraphobia)

Feeling of tightness or heaviness in the chest.

***Effects of Stress on Emotions and Mental Health**

Depression and persistent sadness

***Effects of Stress on Memory and Concentration**

Increased tendency to forget things

Difficulty focusing on tasks

Frequent distraction or restless mind

Feelings of hopelessness and fatigue

Loss of interest in work or daily activities

***Effects of Stress on Behaviour and Relationships**

Irritability and anger over small issues

Tension in personal and social relationships

Frustration or resentment toward others.

3. Scientific Basis of Stress

Stress triggers a biological response in the body and mind.

When we are under stress, the body initiates a natural chemical reaction called the **"fight or flight** "response. **(लड़ो या भागो प्रतिक्रिया)**

This is the body's way of preparing to either confront or escape a perceived threat.

During this response, hormones like cortisol and adrenaline are released.

The body becomes alert, breathing speeds up, and heart rate increases; muscles become tense.

If these hormones are released repeatedly or continuously, the body becomes fatigued, hormonal imbalance occurs, and various illnesses may develop.

4. Effects of Chronic Stress on Health

Diabetes:

Continuous stress can affect blood sugar levels, increasing the risk or worsening diabetes.

Hypertension:

It can lead to hypertension (high blood pressure).

Thyroid:

problems, especially in women, may develop.

Hormonal imbalances:

can cause irregular periods and reduced fertility.

Alzheimer's:

Long-term mental fatigue may contribute to serious conditions like Alzheimer's disease and other chronic illnesses.

5. Case Study:

Name: Ajay Garg

Age: 42 years

Profession: IT Professional

Stress Factors:

Constant project deadlines

Sleep deprivation (3–5 hours per night)

Irregular meal times

Outcome / Results: Over 6 months, he lost weight and started losing hair

Experienced sudden chest pain; hospitalized

Diagnosed with high blood pressure and anxiety

Doctor's Advice: Taking action earlier could have made life much easier.

6. Self-Check:

Is Stress Affecting Your Body and Mind?

Pay attention to the following signs regularly:

Daily Stress Self-Check

Instructions: Tick "Yes" or "No" for each statement:

1. I wake up feeling heavy or restless. ☐ Yes ☐ No
2. I feel tired all the time. ☐ Yes ☐ No
3. My mind feels sad or low without reason. ☐ Yes ☐ No
4. My sleep is light or insufficient. ☐ Yes ☐ No
5. I get upset or frustrated over small things. ☐ Yes ☐ No

How to Interpret:

Yes to 3 or more: Stress may be significantly affecting your body and mind.

Yes to 1–2: Mild stress—watch for patterns and take preventive measures.

No to all: Stress levels are likely manageable, but maintain healthy routines.

7. Step Towards a Solution:

***Awareness**

The first step in managing stress is recognition and acceptance.

What we acknowledge, we can change.

Ignoring the effects of stress is unfair to yourself.

If you start listening to the language of your body and mind, they can guide you toward ways to heal and recover.

Conclusion:

Understanding Chronic Stress

Chronic stress acts like a slow-acting poison, gradually weakening the mind's strength.

You need to become aware of its invisible effects, which silently take away your energy and well-being.

Relieving Stress: Practical Measures and Techniques

"Stress is a situation; the solution is a decision."

Now we have understood what stress is, its causes, and how it affects our body and mind.

It is now time to take the first step toward a solution.

By adopting practical strategies, you can manage, reduce, and even prevent stress from negatively affecting your body and mind.

We will learn some practical techniques that you can apply in your daily life immediately, without any major expense or special equipment.

1. "Breath is peace."

Deep breathing is a key technique to calm the mind and body.

Deep Breathing Technique

Purpose: To calm the mind, reduce stress, and relax the body.

Steps:

1. Sit or lie down in a comfortable position.

2. Close your eyes and relax your shoulders and body.
3. Inhale slowly and deeply through your nose, filling your lungs completely.
4. Hold your breath for 2–3 seconds.
5. Exhale slowly and completely through your mouth.
6. Repeat this process 5–10 times, focusing on the breath.
7. Observe how your mind and body feel calmer and more relaxed.

Tip: Practice this technique daily, especially during stressful moments, to reduce tension and anxiety.

Anulom Vilom Pranayama (Alternate Nostril Breathing)

Purpose:

Balances the mind and body

Reduces stress and anxiety

Improves concentration and lung function

Steps:

1. Sit in a comfortable position with a straight spine.
2. Close your eyes and relax your body.

3. Using your right thumb, gently close your right nostril.
4. Inhale slowly and deeply through your left nostril.
5. Close your left nostril with your ring finger and release the right nostril.
6. Exhale slowly and completely through the right nostril.
7. Inhale deeply through the right nostril.
8. Close the right nostril and exhale through the left nostril.
9. This completes one round.
10. Repeat 5–10 rounds, gradually increasing with practice.

Tips:

Practice on an empty stomach or at least 2–3 hours after meals.

Focus on smooth, deep breaths and remain relaxed throughout.

Benefit of Anulom Vilom Pranayama:

It balances the two hemispheres of the brain, promoting mental clarity, calmness, and emotional stability.

2. Guided Meditation for Stress Relief

What is Guided Meditation?

Guided meditation involves following instructions from an expert or app to focus your mind, relax your body, and reduce stress.

Where to Access:

Available on mobile apps and YouTube.

Offered in simple Hindi, English, and other languages.

Benefits:

Special sessions are designed to reduce stress.

Practicing regularly for 21 days can significantly improve mental clarity, calmness, and emotional balance.

Tips for Practice:

1. Choose a quiet, comfortable place.
2. Use headphones for better focus if needed.
3. Follow the guided instructions slowly and mindfully.
4. Practice daily for best results.

3. Balanced Daily Routine for Stress Management

***Divide Your Day into Three Parts:**

Work Time: Focus on professional or personal tasks efficiently.

Rest and Meal Times: Include proper meals, short breaks, and time to relax.

Family and Social Time: Spend quality moments with loved ones to recharge emotionally.

***Morning Routine:**

Start your day calmly and peacefully.

Avoid checking your phone immediately after waking up.

Spend 5 minutes on deep breathing, meditation, or gentle stretching.

***Time Management:**

Create a daily schedule or timetable.

Assign specific times for work, meals, rest, and social activities.

Follow your schedule consistently to maintain a sense of balance and reduce stress.

***Evening Routine:**

Wind down gradually before bedtime.

Avoid stressful tasks or electronic devices at least 30–60 minutes before sleep.

Reflect on the day positively and plan calmly for the next day.

***Additional Tips:**

Include short breaks during work to relax your mind.

Practice mindfulness or meditation during breaks.

Maintain consistent sleep patterns for better energy and focus.

Mental Resilience: Thought Detox and Replacement Techniques

1. Thought Detox

Purpose: To cleanse negative thinking and cultivate a positive mindset.

Steps:

*Identify negative thoughts such as:

"I can't do this."

"This is beyond me."

"I will never succeed."

*Replace them with positive statements:

"I can do this."

"I am making an effort."

"I am improving every day."

*Practice daily by writing down positive thoughts and repeating them to strengthen confidence and reduce negativity.

2. Thought Replacement Technique

Purpose: To immediately counter negative thoughts with positive ones.

Steps:

1. Notice the negative thought as soon as it arises.
2. Mentally say: "Stop!" to pause the thought.
3. Immediately replace it with a positive statement, for example:

Instead of "I will fail," say "I am learning and improving every day."

4. Repeat consistently to train your mind.

Benefits:

Reduces negative thinking and self-doubt

Improves focus, motivation, and emotional balance

Strengthens overall mental resilience.

5. Emotional Writing / Journaling

Purpose: To process emotions, reduce stress, and gain clarity.

Practice:

1. **Dedicate 10 minutes daily for journaling.**
2. **Reflect on questions such as:**

What caused me stress today?

What good things did I do today?

What can I do differently or better tomorrow?

3. Write freely, expressing your thoughts and feelings without judgment.

Benefits:

Helps organize and clarify thoughts

Reduces mental pressure and tension

Provides emotional relief and a sense of lightness.

6. Self-Care: Befriend Yourself

Make it a habit to gift yourself a few moments each day—

Immerse in your favourite music

Converse with plants or birds

Nourish your mind with books

Refresh your body with a warm bath

Learn to Say No

Remember, not every responsibility is yours to bear.

Set healthy boundaries, and do it without guilt—because protecting your peace is also an act of strength.

7. Physical Exercise: Movement Drives Stress Away

When the body moves, the mind feels lighter.

Regular physical activity not only strengthens your body but also helps chase away stress and restore balance.

Brisk walk:

Walk at a brisk pace for at least 30 minutes daily in fresh, open air.

Practice yoga:

Especially postures like Shavasana, Balasana, Vajrasana—to relax the body and calm the mind.

Dance and sports:

Engage in sports, light workouts, or any form of movement you enjoy.

Make sure to dedicate at least three days a week to physical activities you truly love, as consistency is the key to both health and happiness.

8. Social Connection: Break the Barrier of Loneliness

Don't hold your feelings inside—share your heart with a trusted friend or family member.

Reach out and help others; kindness not only uplifts them but also fills you with deep inner peace.

When you support someone, your own struggles feel lighter, reminding you that none of us are truly alone.

9. Connection with Nature: A Natural Stress Reliever

Spend at least ten minutes in the open air every day.

Sit under a tree, gaze at the sky, or listen to the songs of birds.

Scientific studies confirm that nature naturally reduces stress, bringing calmness to the mind and healing to the heart.

10. Distance from Technology: Embrace a Digital Detox

Give yourself the gift of an hour without your phone after waking up—let your mind start the day calmly.

Similarly, avoid screens for an hour before bedtime, allowing your mind and body to rest fully.

Set limits on social media to protect yourself from negativity and information overload.

By reducing screen time mindfully, you create space to reflect, recharge, and truly connect with yourself and the world around you.

11. Inspiring Example:

Name: Minaxi

Age: 36

Profession: Teacher

Situation:

Minaxi was feeling overwhelmed with work pressure at school, responsibilities of her children's studies, and challenges related to her husband's job.

Steps Taken:

Practiced 15 minutes of meditation every morning.

Dedicated every Sunday evening to a mobile-free family time.

Took up gardening as a relaxing hobby.

Learned to say no and set healthy boundaries.

Result:

Within three months, Minaxi experienced improved sleep, and her face regained its natural glow.

She felt more balanced, peaceful, and energized in her daily life.

12. Self-Check:

Am I Moving in the Right Direction?

Take a moment each week to reflect:

_Have I taken meaningful time for myself?

_Are my breaths slow, deep, and calming?

_Am I nurturing positive thoughts in my mind?

_Can I set boundaries and say no, without carrying guilt?

_Remember, these simple reflections help you stay aligned with your well-being and personal growth.

Conclusion:

Overcoming stress may seem challenging, but it is far from impossible. Even small, consistent actions can create profound change over time.

There is no **magic wand** required—

just your intention, a little discipline, and the habit of practicing self-care regularly.

Remember, every step you take toward your well-being brings you closer to a calmer, happier, and more balanced life.

Stress in Special Situations – Exams, Jobs, Relationships, and Life Challenges

"In every situation, stress arises depending on how a person perceives it and on their ability to handle it."

For students, examinations are one of the most common sources of stress. The pressure to perform well, expectations from parents and teachers, and fear of failure often lead to anxiety. At the workplace, employees may experience stress due to deadlines, workload, or job insecurity. In personal relationships and family life, conflicts and misunderstandings can also create emotional strain. However, by adopting the right strategies, these pressures can be managed effectively.

1. Exam and Study Stress

Major Causes:

*Fear of results

*Pressure of expectations from self and others

*Lack of proper time management.

*Anxiety about not meeting academic or personal goals.

Causes:

*Pressure of targets and deadlines

*Lack of coordination among colleagues

*Job insecurity

*Work–life imbalance

Possible Solutions:

*Proper planning and systematic preparation.

*Keeping the mind calm and relaxed through breaks and mindfulness.

*Maintaining a balanced and nutritious diet.

*Practicing positive thinking and self-confidence-building exercises.

*Divide study into intervals (Pomodoro Technique – 25 minutes study, 5 minutes break).

*Stay away from distractions like mobile phones and social media.

*Follow a healthy diet and daily routine.

*Don't overthink about results – focus only on efforts.

*Practice meditation and breathing exercises for concentration.

Example Case:

Amit, a 17-year-old student, constantly feared failing his board exams. Even during meals, he worried about the results. His anxiety led to headaches and sleepless nights. With guidance, Amit made a to-do list, divided subjects into smaller parts, and practiced daily meditation. Gradually, his confidence improved, and he performed well in exams without feeling overwhelmed.

2. Stress in Relationships – Family and Social

Main Causes:

*Lack of communication

*Misunderstandings

*Financial problems

*External interference

Effects:

*Frequent arguments

*Silence and distance in relationships

*Blaming each other

*Negative impact on children and family environment

Solutions:

*Mutual understanding and acceptance – respecting each other's perspective.

*Develop a "we" mindset instead of an "I" mindset to strengthen togetherness.

*If needed, seek help from a counselor for professional guidance.

*Spend quality time together without mobile phones or digital distractions.

*When angry, remain silent for a while, calm yourself first, and then communicate peacefully.

Example Case:

Priya and Karan, married for 10 years, often fought over financial matters. Their arguments created silence at home, affecting their children's mood. Realizing the pattern, they began setting aside 30 minutes daily without phones just to talk. They also met a family counselor who guided them in healthy communication. Slowly, their bond grew stronger, and the home atmosphere became peaceful again.

Job and Career-Related Stress

Main Causes:

*Job insecurity

*Conflicts with boss or colleagues

*Excessive workload

*Pressure of promotions or salary expectations

*Lack of work–life balance

Symptoms:

*Irritability and mood swings

*Frequent headaches

*Anxiety or nervousness about work

*Carrying mental burden even during holidays

*Self-doubt, feeling “I am not good enough”

Possible Solutions:

*Set realistic goals and break tasks into smaller steps

*Set priorities by preparing a to-do list and completing tasks step by step.

*Maintain clear and respectful communication with colleagues.

*Practice relaxation techniques such as meditation and deep breathing.

*Ensure proper rest, exercise, and a healthy lifestyle to maintain balance.

*If needed, seek career counseling to gain clarity and direction in professional life.

Example Case:

Riya, a 32-year-old marketing executive, loved her job and worked hard to prove herself. After a big promotion, her responsibilities increased sharply — long hours, constant deadlines, and no time for rest.

Soon, she started feeling exhausted, irritable, and anxious. Headaches and sleepless nights became common. Despite success, she felt unhappy and disconnected from family and friends.

On her doctor's advice, Riya took a short break and began practicing time management, saying "no" when necessary, and spending time on self-care. Gradually, her stress reduced, and she regained her confidence.

Lesson: Success loses meaning when health and peace are lost — balance is the true achievement.

Stress During Major Life Transitions

(Death, Divorce, Breakup, or Financial Crisis)

Main Causes:

*Sudden emptiness in life

*Fear of the future

*Feelings of guilt or self-blame

*Social pressure and stigma

Symptoms:

*Deep sadness and loneliness

*Disturbances in sleep and appetite

*Hopelessness or feelings of "everything is over"

*Occasional thoughts of self-harm or suicide

Solutions:

*Express grief openly – cry, write, or talk to someone you trust.

*Gradually build a new daily routine to bring stability.

*Seek support from a therapist or counselor – it is not weakness, but wisdom.

*Join support groups and connect with people who have gone through similar experiences.

*Keep reminding yourself: **"This too shall pass."**

Example Case

Radhika, a 38-year-old woman, went through a painful divorce after 12 years of marriage. Suddenly, her life felt empty and uncertain. She struggled with loneliness, sleepless nights, and constant self-doubt— "Was it my fault?" She even felt hopeless about her future.

With time, Radhika began to express her emotions by writing in a journal and sharing her feelings with a close friend. She also sought help from a professional counselor, who guided her to rebuild her confidence. Gradually, she created a new routine—morning walks, focusing on her work, and joining a support group of women who had faced similar challenges.

Today, Radhika admits the pain was real, but so was her strength. She often reminds herself, "That difficult time has passed, and I am stronger because of it."

5 S Formula – For Situations and Stress Management

1. S – Accept (Svikar / Accept the Situation)

Instead of denying or ignoring the situation, acknowledge it.

Example: "Yes, this is a challenging situation, but I need to understand it."

2. S – Understand (Samjhein / Understand the Cause)

Identify the root cause of stress or the problem.

Example: "Why am I feeling stressed? Is it work pressure, relationships, or fear of the future?"

3. S – Share / Seek Support (Saazhaa / Share)

Talk to a trusted person or expert; express your thoughts.

Example: Confiding in a friend, family member, or mental health professional.

4. S – Stabilize / Balance (Santulan / Create Balance)

Align your emotions and actions; maintain inner equilibrium.

Example: Practicing deep breathing, yoga, or time management to balance mind and body.

5. S – Step Towards Solution (Samadhan / Take Action)

Take practical steps while keeping your thoughts and emotions in check.

Example: Making a task list, setting small goals, or solving the problem step by step.

Here's a quick, one-line 5S mantra you can use anytime:

"Accept it, Understand it, Share it, Balance it, Solve it."

*Short, easy to remember.

*Covers the full 5S process.

*Can be silently repeated when feeling stressed to regain clarity and control.

Conclusion:

"Certainly, every situation can be stressful, but in every situation, stress can also be managed positively.

Remember: 'Different situations, different solutions.'

Just as a doctor prescribes a different medicine for each illness, similarly, the approach for each stressful situation needs to be different."

"Stress is often overlooked in both children and the elderly"

It is not just a problem of older adults—behind innocent faces and bent backs, unspoken pains often lie hidden. We tend to assume that children and older people lead worry-free lives, but the reality is far different. Stress manifests itself in unique ways at every age."

"Children can feel stressed for many reasons:

the pressure of studies and exams, high expectations from parents, constant comparisons with friends, family problems like divorce, and the pressures of social media and cyberbullying. These factors can quietly weigh on their young minds, often going unnoticed."

"Symptoms of stress in children:

*may include becoming suddenly withdrawn,

*losing interest in studies, changes in sleep and eating habits, irritability, moodiness, stomach-aches, headaches, or other physical complaints without any apparent medical cause."

Solutions:

Keep communication with children open and loving.

Spend at least 15 minutes a day talking with them without giving instructions or criticism. Encourage play and creative activities, instead of focusing only on academics. Appreciate their efforts, not just the results. Promote digital awareness by setting limits on social media use and monitoring their activity.

If needed, consult a child psychologist for guidance.

Causes of Stress in Adolescents:

Stress in teenagers can arise from identity exploration, physical changes during puberty, career and future concerns, relationship issues, and comparisons on social media.

Symptoms:

Mood swings, withdrawal, intense desire for independence, social isolation, and risky behaviours such as substance use.

Solutions:

Listen more, give less advice.

Allow them to express themselves freely. Be a role model—teach through your own example, not just by preaching. Balance independence with responsibility. Let them make small decisions on their own. Promote mental health awareness, treating it as a normal topic—there is no shame in discussing it.

Stress in the Elderly:

The main causes of stress among older adults include loneliness, (children being busy or living apart)

health problems, financial insecurity,

feelings of uselessness such as "I am no longer needed,"

the loss of a life partner, and the absence of friends' companionship.

Symptoms:

sadness, withdrawal, insomnia,

memory problems, feelings of hopelessness, irritability or stubborn behaviour

self-blame and a sense that life has lost its meaning.

Solutions:

Show love not just through money, but through your presence.

Take care of their health through regular check-ups, medication, yoga, and other practices.

Encourage social engagement by connecting with senior centres or social clubs.

Learn digital skills, such as using mobile phones and video calls, to stay connected with everyone.

Adjust your own behaviour—avoid always speaking in an authoritative manner.

Their time has passed, and now it is the younger generation's time.

By adapting your thoughts and behaviour according to the times, stress can be reduced. Understand the generational gap to foster better relationships.

Example Case:

Child (10 years old):

Rohan has been feeling anxious and withdrawn. His grades started slipping, and he avoids talking to his parents. He spends more time on his phone, comparing himself with friends on social media.

Causes: Academic pressure, high parental expectations, peer comparisons, social media influence.

Symptoms: Withdrawal, loss of interest in studies, irritability, disrupted sleep.

Solution: His parents started spending 20 minutes daily talking with him without giving instructions, encouraged him to play and engage in creative activities, and praised his efforts rather than only his grades. They limited his social media time and monitored his online activity.

Adolescent (16 years old):

Priya feels stressed and frustrated. She argues often with her parents, feels pressure to decide on her career path, and experiences mood swings.

Causes: Identity exploration, puberty changes, future and career concerns, peer and social media pressures.

Symptoms: Mood swings, desire for independence, social withdrawal, occasional risky behaviours.

Solution: Her parents listened actively, involved her in small family decisions, and modelled balanced behaviour. Priya was allowed to make some decisions on her own, and discussions about mental health were normalized.

3. Elderly:

Mr. Sharma, aged 70, felt lonely after his spouse passed away. He worried about finances and felt disconnected from his children, who were busy with their own families.

Causes: Loneliness, health issues, loss of spouse, financial insecurity, social isolation.

Symptoms: Sadness, insomnia, withdrawal, feelings of uselessness, hopelessness.

Solution: His children involved him in small family decisions, encouraged him to join a social club, and helped him learn to use video calls to connect with relatives. They supported him in maintaining health routines like yoga and regular check-ups. They also adjusted their communication style, avoiding constant instructions and speaking in a more participative manner. Over time, Mr. Sharma felt more valued, socially connected, and emotionally supported.

Conclusion:

Stress affects individuals differently across all age groups, from children to adolescents to the elderly. Understanding the causes, recognizing symptoms, and applying age-appropriate solutions—such as open communication, active participation, encouragement, and social engagement—can significantly reduce stress and improve overall well-being.

Five Key Principles to Handle Stress in Children and the Elderly:

1. **Listen:**

   Hear them out completely without interrupting.

2. **Presence:**

   Build trust and reassurance through your presence.

3. **Appreciation:**

   Appreciate their small efforts and achievements.

4. **Freedom:**

   Give them space to express themselves without pressure.

5. **Counselling:**

   Seek professional help when necessary.

Conclusion:

Stress in both children and the elderly often goes unnoticed because they speak little or cannot express themselves.

However, sometimes some elderly talk excessively and remain constantly authoritative, which can distance them from their families.

If we stay alert, learn to read emotions, and take timely and appropriate actions, we can fill lives with happiness.

A smiling childhood and a respected old age are the true hallmarks of a healthy society.

21-Day Action Plan for a Stress-Free Life

"Small-small systematic steps can bring big changes in life"

If you make a new beginning every day with small efforts, gradually these efforts bring remarkable changes in your mental, emotional, and behavioural life.

That's why—this 21-day special plan is designed with small but effective activities that will slowly free you from stress and bring you towards balance.

Special features of the action plan:

Every day, a new activity.

*Simple habits that can be easily included in daily life.

*Practical, effective, and meaningful exercises.

*Easy steps towards a balanced and stress-free life.

21-Day Action Plan

Day 1: Beginning with Silence

Practice 5 minutes of complete silence every morning after waking up.

No phone, no conversation with anyone—just experience the silence of your own mind.

Why it matters:

Silence gives your mind a fresh start. It helps you connect with yourself before the noise of the day takes over.

How to practice:

1. After waking up, sit in a comfortable position.
2. Close your eyes and spend 5 minutes in complete silence.
3. Do not touch your phone or speak to anyone during this time.
4. Just notice your breathing and allow your mind to settle.

Reflection/ Benefit:

This short practice will calm your nervous system, make your thoughts clearer, and give you a peaceful beginning for the day.

Day 2: Write a Gratitude List

Every morning, write down five things/people/events you feel grateful for.

This small habit will give your mind peace and emotional stability.

Why it matters:

Gratitude shifts your focus from what is missing to what is already good in life. This reduces stress and increases happiness.

How to practice:

1. Keep a small notebook beside your bed.
2. Every morning, write down 5 things, people, or experiences you are thankful for.
3. They can be big (family, career) or small (a good meal, a smile, fresh air).

Reflection/Benefit:

Writing gratitude daily builds positivity, emotional balance, and resilience against stress.

Day 3: Write down 4 things

Write down four tasks that you don't want to postpone but have been delaying.

Completing these small pending tasks gives you a big sense of relief.

Why it matters:

Unfinished tasks create hidden stress in the mind. Every time you delay them, they occupy mental space. Completing them gives a sense of relief and control.

How to practice:

1. Write down 4 small tasks you've been postponing.

Example: replying to an email, organizing a drawer, calling a relative, paying a bill.

2. Choose at least 1 and complete it today.

3. Keep repeating this until all 4 tasks are done within 1–2 days.

Reflection/Benefit:

You'll feel instant relief and satisfaction. By clearing small tasks, you reduce hidden stress and build confidence to handle bigger challenges.

Day 5: Breathing Practice

Close your eyes, sit quietly, and take deep breaths for 5 minutes (Breath Meditation).

Why it matters:

Stress often shows up in shallow breathing. Deep breathing signals safety to your brain, calms anxiety, and improves oxygen flow in the body.

How to practice:

1. Sit comfortably, close your eyes, and place one hand on your chest and one on your stomach.
2. Inhale slowly through your nose for 4 counts.
3. Hold the breath for 2 counts.

4. Exhale slowly through your mouth for 6 counts.
5. Repeat this cycle for 5 minutes.

Reflection/Benefit:

This simple breathing technique will instantly relax your muscles, slow down racing thoughts, and restore inner balance.

Day 6: Digital Detox Hour

Keep at least one hour completely free from mobile, TV, and social media.

Spend this time with family, or in nature, or in complete relaxation.

Why it matters:

Constant screen time overstimulates the brain and increases stress hormones. A digital detox gives rest to your eyes, mind, and emotions.

How to practice:

1. Choose one hour of the day (morning, evening, or before sleep) where you avoid all screens—phone, TV, computer.
2. Use this time to connect with family, read, cook, meditate, or simply relax.
3. Inform people if needed, so you don't feel pressured to reply immediately.

Reflection/Benefit:

You'll feel calmer, more present, and more connected with yourself and your surroundings. Sleep and focus will also improve.

Day 7: Practice Forgiveness

Forgive someone in your heart who has hurt you in the past.

This forgiveness is for your own peace and mental freedom.

You can also write down on paper: "I forgive ___ for ___." Then tear the paper. This will bring emotional relief.

Why it matters:

Holding on to past hurt keeps your mind in stress mode. Forgiveness is not about excusing others—it's about freeing yourself from emotional burden.

How to practice:

1. Think of someone who has hurt you and still occupies your mind.
2. Write on a piece of paper: "I forgive [Name] for [situation]. I release this pain."
3. Read it aloud gently, then tear or discard the paper.
4. Say to yourself: "I choose peace over anger."

Reflection/Benefit:

You will feel lighter emotionally. Forgiveness brings inner peace, lowers resentment, and helps you move forward with more freedom.

Day 8: Express Appreciation

Compliment someone honestly for their good qualities or work.

Small words of appreciation create big happiness in relationships.

Why it matters:

Stress often makes us focus on flaws and mistakes in others. Appreciation, on the other hand, creates positivity in relationships and strengthens emotional bonds.

How to practice:

1. Choose one person—family, friend, or colleague.
2. Notice one quality, effort, or action you genuinely value in them.
3. Express it honestly: "I really appreciate how you always support me" or "Thank you for your kindness today."
4. Make it specific rather than general.

Reflection/Benefit:

This small habit builds warmth and trust in relationships. You'll feel happier, and the other person will feel valued—creating a positive ripple effect.

Day 9: Affirmations

Choose one affirmation, for example:

"I am calm. I will not let stress overpower me. I will handle every situation with peace."

Repeat this affirmation many times throughout the day.

Why it matters:

Negative self-talk feeds stress. Affirmations rewire your brain to believe in calmness, confidence, and inner strength.

How to practice:

1. Choose one affirmation that feels meaningful to you, such as:

"I am calm and in control."

"I release stress and welcome peace."

"I can handle challenges with strength."

2. Repeat it several times in the morning, during the day, and before sleep.

3. Write it on sticky notes and place them where you can see them.

Reflection/Benefit:

Repeating affirmations daily reduces negative thinking. Over time, you'll naturally feel calmer and more confident.

Day 10: Nature Walk

Spend at least 15 minutes walking in the open air, garden, or park.

During this time, observe and feel nature mindfully.

Why it matters:

Nature lowers stress hormones, improves mood, and restores mental energy. Even a short time outdoors can work like therapy.

How to practice:

1. Go for a 15-minute walk in a park, garden, or open space.
2. While walking, notice details: the sound of birds, colors of leaves, fresh air.
3. Walk slowly and mindfully, without rushing or using your phone.

Reflection/Benefit:

Nature will relax your mind, clear mental fatigue, and give you a fresh perspective. You'll return feeling lighter and more alive.

Day 11: Write Down Your Emotions

Whatever emotions are inside you—positive or negative—write them down honestly in a diary.

Writing makes your inner world lighter and helps you understand yourself better.

Why it matters:

Unexpressed emotions build stress inside the mind and body. Writing is a safe outlet to release feelings and understand them better.

How to practice:

1. Take 10 minutes at night to journal your emotions.
2. Write freely without worrying about grammar or style.
3. Ask yourself: "What did I feel today? What made me happy? What stressed me?"
4. End with one positive note, such as: **"I am proud that I handled today."**

Reflection/Benefit:

Journaling clears mental clutter, reduces anxiety, and helps you gain insight into your own emotional patterns.

Day 12: One Hour Without Complaints

For one hour, avoid complaining about anything.

Notice how often you complain and how much unnecessary negativity it creates in both mind and body.

Why it matters:

Complaining reinforces negativity in the brain. Reducing complaints shifts focus to problem-solving and positivity.

How to practice:

1. Choose one hour today to consciously avoid complaining.
2. If a complaint arises, reframe it into a neutral or positive statement. Example: instead of "Traffic is terrible," say "I have time to listen to music in the car."
3. Notice how often you tend to complain unconsciously.

Reflection/Benefit:

This practice will make you more mindful of your words and thoughts. Over time, it reduces negativity and builds resilience.

Day 13: Learn from Inspiration

Read or listen to an inspirational story or biography.

Watch a motivational video or TED Talk.

Why it matters:

Hearing stories of people who overcame struggles gives us courage and hope. Inspiration reminds us that stress is temporary and growth is possible.

How to practice:

1. Read a short biography, watch a motivational video, or listen to a podcast.
2. Focus on how the person handled challenges and what you can learn.
3. Write down one key takeaway and apply it in your own life.

Reflection/Benefit:

Inspirational stories uplift your spirit, expand your perspective, and remind you of your own strength.

Day 14: Deep Breathing (Thrice a Day)

Practice deep breathing 3 times daily (morning, afternoon, evening) for 10 minutes.

It refreshes mind and body instantly.

Why it matters:

Breathing deeply at different times of the day prevents stress from building up. It's like pressing the refresh button for your mind and body.

How to practice:

1. Set reminders for morning, afternoon, and evening.
2. Each time, sit comfortably and close your eyes.
3. Inhale deeply through your nose, hold for 2–3 seconds, and exhale slowly.
4. Repeat for 5–10 minutes.

Reflection/Benefit:

This routine lowers stress throughout the day, boosts focus, and helps you maintain calm energy in all situations.

Day 15: Goal Visualization

Sit quietly and visualize your goal as if it is already accomplished.

Example: imagine the joy and relief of reaching your desired result.

Visualization strengthens confidence and motivates you to act.

Why it matters:

Stress often comes from uncertainty about the future. Visualization creates mental clarity, builds confidence, and motivates you to act toward your goals.

How to practice:

1. Sit quietly in a calm place.

2. Close your eyes and imagine one important goal as if it is already achieved.
3. Picture yourself in detail—your emotions, surroundings, and the success.
4. Feel the joy, relief, and pride in that moment.

Reflection/Benefit:

Visualization programs your brain for success. You will feel hopeful, motivated, and less fearful about the future.

Day 16: Help Someone Else

Do one act of kindness or service without expecting anything in return.

Even a small help—listening to someone, giving encouragement, or offering support—creates positivity in both hearts.

Why it matters:

Acts of kindness reduce stress hormones and increase feelings of connection. Helping others shifts focus away from your own worries.

How to practice:

1. Do one act of kindness today—listen to someone, encourage them, or help with a small task.
2. Do it without expecting anything in return.
3. Pay attention to how the other person feels after your action.

Reflection/Benefit:

Helping others creates joy in both hearts. You'll feel lighter, more connected, and emotionally enriched.

Day 17: Learn Something New

Spend some time learning something new today.

It could be reading a new topic, practicing a new skill, or trying a new hobby.

Learning keeps the brain active and fresh.

Why it matters:

Learning keeps the brain flexible, curious, and alive. It prevents boredom, builds confidence, and adds excitement to daily life.

How to practice:

1. Pick a small new skill, hobby, or topic you've always wanted to explore.

   Example: cooking a new dish, learning a phrase in another language, practicing a craft.

2. Dedicate 15–20 minutes today to learn it.

3. Celebrate even small progress.

Reflection/Benefit:

You'll feel refreshed and energized. Learning new things enhances self-esteem and makes life more enjoyable.

Day 18: Self-Reflection

Write a short reflection on where you see yourself after six months.

Note your goals and dreams clearly.

This helps in creating direction and focus.

Why it matters:

Stress often comes from living without direction. Reflection brings clarity about what matters most and where you want to go.

How to practice:

1. Take 15 minutes with a notebook and pen.
2. Write down: "Where do I see myself in 6 months?"
3. Note your personal, emotional, and professional goals.
4. Keep your notes safe and revisit them often.

Reflection/Benefit:

You will gain focus and direction. Knowing your goals reduces confusion and brings confidence in handling challenges.

Day 19: Change Your Environment

Rearrange something in your surroundings.

For example: organize your desk, room, or any small corner differently.

Small environmental changes refresh the mind and improve creativity.

Why it matters:

A cluttered or stagnant environment adds to stress. Small physical changes refresh the mind and stimulate creativity.

How to practice:

1. Choose one small space—your desk, room, or cupboard.
2. Rearrange, clean, or add something new (like a plant or photo).
3. Notice how your mood changes afterward.

Reflection/Benefit:

You'll feel refreshed, creative, and lighter. A changed environment inspires new energy and positivity.

Day 20: Recreational Activity

Do any activity that gives you happiness and relaxation—listen to music, sing, dance, paint, garden, or spend time with a hobby.

Such activities refresh your mind and bring joy into your daily routine.

Why it matters:

Fun and relaxation are not luxuries—they are essential for a healthy mind. Recreational activities release tension and awaken joy.

How to practice:

1. Choose an activity you truly enjoy—music, dancing, painting, gardening, or any hobby.
2. Spend at least 20–30 minutes on it today.
3. Do it purely for enjoyment, without focusing on results.

Reflection/Benefit:

Your stress will melt away, and you'll feel playful and recharged. Recreation balances seriousness with joy in life.

Day 21: A Fresh Beginning with Gratitude

Spend a few minutes reflecting with gratitude—towards your body, mind, and family.

End the 21-day plan by silently thanking yourself and life.

From here, start the journey of a balanced and mindful lifestyle.

Why it matters:

The end of this 21-day journey is also a beginning. Gratitude seals your progress and strengthens your commitment to a balanced life.

How to practice:

1. Sit in silence for a few minutes.
2. Think of your body, mind, family, and life, and silently thank them.
3. Write down 3 ways you will continue practicing stress-free living beyond these 21 days.

Reflection/Benefit:

You'll feel fulfilled and peaceful. Gratitude anchors happiness, while commitment ensures that these practices stay in your life.

🌸 Conclusion

Stress-free living is not a miracle—it's the result of consistent small steps.

These 21 days are only the beginning. By continuing these practices, you will experience deep peace, resilience, and lasting joy.

📝 Daily Self-Reflection Journal

Today's Date: __________

Day: __________

1. How did I practice today's activity?

✍

____

____

2. What emotions did I feel before starting the activity?

✍

____

____

3. What emotions did I feel after completing the activity?

✍

____

____

4. What stress or worries did I notice in myself today?

✍

____

____

5. What is one thing I am grateful for today?

6. How will I continue applying this practice tomorrow?

Stress to Solution: The Final Word

"Stress is not the end of life; it is the first sign of change."

It is not the conclusion of a journey, but the beginning of a new path.

In this book, you have explored chapter by chapter:

*What stress is, why it occurs, and how it grows

*Its physical and mental effects

*Challenges of modern life

*Unique aspects of stress among different groups and ages

*Ways to manage it—through yoga, meditation, communication, and self-awareness

*A 21-day transformation journey to practice positive change

Stress is Your Friend; Stress is not a disaster.

*It does not halt the flow of life; it signals you to pay attention.

*Sometimes it reveals your limitations, sometimes it uncovers your possibilities.

*Stress is the moment of choice—

where you either break or grow stronger.

The power is in your hands:

Will you rise, or will you fall apart?

Ask Yourself

Whenever stress arises, ask ::

*How am I perceiving this?

*Is there an opportunity hidden within it?

*Is it signalling me to pause and rethink?

*The solution always lies within.

*Books, teachers, and friends can guide you, but lasting resolution comes only when you turn inward.

*The answer to stress is not outside—it is within.

Daily Guidelines for a Balanced Life:

*Begin each day with silence and gratitude.

*Engage in honest conversations.

*Do not hesitate to say **"no"** when needed.

*Find joy in the little things.

*Seek professional counselor help if necessary.

*Dedicate some time for yourself every week.

*Above all, love yourself.

A humble request:

*Continue, share, and put into practice what you have learned.

*Even a single word or habit from you may bring growth and inspiration to someone else's life.

A New Beginning

This is not the final page—it is the first step toward a life that is balanced, peaceful, and meaningful.

You are the author of your own life.

Now, the pen is in your hand to turn stress into solutions.

Peace does not lie outside—it begins within.

This journey of discovery begins today, here and now.

Dear Reader,

If this book has helped you even in a small way to understand and manage stress, then my purpose has been fulfilled. I humbly request you not to keep the insights and techniques shared here to yourself, but to pass them on to your family, friends, and community.

Stress has become a shared burden in today's world — and its solution lies in collective awareness and mutual support.

Let us together take a step toward better mental health and emotional empowerment.

Your feedback, suggestions, and experiences are precious to me. Please feel free to share them — so this journey may continue and touch more lives.

Your participation is a contribution to the well-being of all.

– Dr. Rekha Gaur